HMO LANDLORD RULES

Proven Strategies to Increase Your Income from Multi-Let Property Investing

C. J. Haliburton

BA DMS Cert

Experienced HMO landlord with over 100 HMOs and 800 tenants

www.hmodaddy.com

Copyright 2014 C. J. Haliburton

www.hmodaddy.com

The moral right of the author has been asserted.

All rights reserved. Apart from any fair dealing for the purposes of research, or private study, or criticism, or review, as permitted under the Copyright, Designs and Patents Act 1988, this publication may only be reproduced, stored or transmitted, in any form or by any means, with the prior permission in writing of the copyright owner, or in the case of the reprographic reproduction in accordance with the terms of licences issued by the Copyright Licensing Agency. Enquiries concerning reproduction outside those terms should be sent to the publisher.

HMO Daddy
14 Walsall Road
Wednesbury
West Midlands
WS10 9JL

Print Edition
ISBN: 978-1-326-12448-9
British Library Cataloguing in Publication Data.
A catalogue record for this book is available from the British Library.

Cover design and editing by Oxford Literary Consultancy

Contents

Introduction 7
Rule 1: Just do it 9
Rule 2: An HMO needs at least five tenants 9
Rule 3: An HMO grosses three times more than a single-let 10
Rule 4: Cash release and no money left in 10
Rule 5: The rule of 5 11
Rule 6: Property values double every ten years 12
Rule 7: Keep it professional 12
Rule 8: Give respect 13
Rule 9: Don't expect fair play 14
Rule 10: Be nice to tenants 14
Rule 11: Treat non-payment excuses as lies 15
Rule 12: Serve eviction notice as soon as tenant fails to pay 15
Rule 13: Retaliatory complaints 16
Rule 14: Keep good records 17
Rule 15: Tipping point 18
Rule 16: Believe in yourself 19
Rule 17: Do research carefully 20
Rule 18: Never delay dealing with repairs, abandonment or late payment 21
Rule 19: "I'll have to ask the boss!" 22
Rule 20: The rule of 20 23

Rule 21: Rule of 40/10 23
Rule 22: If you want affection get a dog or cat 24
Rule 23: Tenants aren't friends 25
Rule 24: Don't employ tenants 25
Rule 25: Tenants lie about other tenants 26
Rule 26: Tenants don't complain enough 26
Rule 27: Professionals usually have a hidden agenda 27
Rule 28: Everything is your responsibility 27
Rule 29: Housing benefit is difficult 28
Rule 30: Experts aren't always right 29
Rule 31: Avoid litigation 30
Rule 32: Expect to be scared 30
Rule 33: Get it in writing 31
Rule 34: Treat officials with respect 31
Rule 35: Hone your intuition 32
Rule 36: The truth will out 33
Rule 37: Energy conservation is a con 34
Rule 38: Manage your HMOs yourself 34
Rule 39: Give bad tenants their money back 35
Rule 40: If it's free, it is abused 35
Rule 41: Forget maintenance contracts 36
Rule 42: Fit a fire door 36
Rule 43: Extras make no difference 37
Rule 44: Finding tenants 38

Rule 45: Do not show more than two rooms or properties 38

Rule 46: The longer a tenant stays, the longer they will stay 39

Rule 47: Charge an administration fee 39

Rule 48: Do not increase rents for good tenants 40

Rule 49: Increase rent for problem tenants 41

Rule 50: Do not charge a deposit 41

The Author 43

I want to hear from you 45

Introduction

Welcome to the first edition of *HMO Landlord Rules*. My title is slightly misleading as there are actually no rules to being an HMO landlord. This can be exciting, but it can also be nerve-racking at times, which is why I've written this book.

When I started, I wanted to believe there was a correct way to invest in property. Luckily, as it turned out, there were no courses to teach me how to invest in property. It was only after I had been a landlord for about ten years that such courses started to appear. I went on some of these courses, although due to my experience I am more critical than other less-experienced investors. I still go on courses as I occasionally learn something – but I also question a lot.

I lived in a new housing estate when I first got married and my wife and I would regularly socialise with the neighbours, most of whom were doctors. They instilled in me the discipline of looking for evidence and proof.

The point is: where is the evidence with what works in property? Apart from profit, which is evidence of success, I struggle. I now do joint ventures (JVs), where the JV funds the deal and I do all the work. I have this quaint notion that he who pays the piper, calls the tune, so I do what the JV partner wants, or at least consider it. I have tried things outside my comfort zone – things I would never have done or would not do – and they have worked. I am now even less sure of what you *should* and *should not* do.

It is natural to want rules or want to be told what to do. When I was a lecturer I found that most people learnt better by starting with a set of rules, principles or structure. Then, once you have done this, you give the exceptions. We all need the rules first.

This is how many people's minds work. They cannot cope with uncertainty and they need rules. It gets worse once the rules are established. Many cannot cope with the exceptions. We see what we want and ignore or rubbish anything does not fit into the way things *should* work.

If I had to boil down all I understand about property, then I would summarise it as: doing what you can for maximum income and minimum work. If it works, don't knock it. Residential property has the unique feature of increasing in value so just owning it can give a fantastic return, and if you can let it, an income. You can often borrow all the money to do this. Unbelievable when you sit down and think it through.

The important thing is that when you get into property there is rarely a *good* or *bad* time. You are often only wise in retrospect. I started with the opinion that property would be unlikely to rise in value, so I went for income. That is why I started with HMOs. I was very wrong. My property also increased massively in value. I love being wrong like that.

I hope you enjoy this book and wish you every success.

Jim Haliburton

Rule 1
Just do it

Just do it – you will never be ready. The longer you delay, the harder it will become to start being an HMO landlord. You will also be held back by the good deals you have missed and hope a similar deal will come along. They rarely do. Accept that much in this business is an act of faith. The following questions are unanswerable:

- Will you get tenants?
- Will you get finance?
- Will property prices increase?
- Where will interest rates go to?
- Etc, etc.

You just have to try it!

Rule 2
An HMO needs at least five tenants

An HMO, to be viable, needs to have at least five tenants – though there are exceptions to this rule. The rule goes like this: the first two tenants pay the mortgage, if you have bought using a mortgage or the rent if you are renting. The third tenant pays the bills, i.e. council tax, gas, electricity, water, insurance, etc. The fourth tenant covers maintenance, voids and bad debts. And the fifth tenant is profit. Try and have six or more tenants as all the extra tenants are extra profit. I find it costs the same to operate a four-bed HMO as it does an eight-bed HMO.

Rule 3
An HMO grosses three times more than a single-let

An HMO let by the room grosses three or more times the income of the same property let as a single let – this rule is a rough approximation. It does not apply to areas with high property prices where the margin is far less but the capital appreciation is awesome.

Rule 4
Cash release and no money left in

HMOs can be valued on income – i.e. the gross annual rent is multiplied by a factor of 7 to 12, sometimes more. This is known as the investment value or a commercial valuation. Which multiplier is used is down to the valuer. In areas of reasonably priced properties, this method of valuation will give a cash release as lenders will lend up to 70% of the value (sometimes more or sometimes less) resulting in no money tied up in the property and tax-free cash to spend. Money released from remortgaging a property is treated as a loan and so not taxable.

A lot of people – including mortgage brokers – have difficulty in understanding or believing this rule. I have done this over a hundred times and I am still doing it, so I know it works.

Rule 5
The rule of 5

Use the *rule of 5* to assess whether to buy an HMO. Buy if the purchase price of the property plus the cost of improvements and other costs equal or are less than five times the gross rent. Follow this rule if you can and you will not go far wrong. Unfortunately, not everyone invests in areas of low-cost housing, so to successfully invest in the right areas the alternative way to assess a prospective HMO is to do the income and expenditure calculations for the property very carefully.

Example: property, when converted will house six tenants at £70 pw, gross rent £21,840 (6 tenants x £70 pw rent x 52 weeks in a year). I would not spend more than £110K

(£21,840 x 5) on buying and refurbishing the property.

Rule 6
Property values double every ten years

Property on average doubles every ten years, though the increase in rents is much slower. Property prices and rent are not linked. Is there any other business where the largest working asset cost is fixed when you buy it, yet the income from and the value of the asset increases? In twenty years, a house brought for, say, £100K will be worth £400K, if average price increases are maintained, which they have consistently done since 1900, with a few exceptions. If you assume rents have only doubled, then you will have doubled your return *and* be sitting on a substantial increase in capital value. Reflect on this when the day-to-day niggles, or worse, get you down.

Rule 7
Keep it professional

The next four rules, and many of the others, all have the same theme. You need to be able to stand back, detach yourself from it, and treat it all as a bit of a game – otherwise it will chew you up and spit you out. I am not saying do not care or be concerned. But if you let your emotions become too involved, it will exhaust you and you will be in danger of losing your cool.

Remember the numbers. You will lose some, but take it as a percentage. X percentage of tenants will not pay or cause damage, and the same goes for tradesmen, etc. With careful management you can keep it to a small percentage, so it does not matter. Look at it as a cost of doing business. Keep in mind the bigger picture (see Rules 20 and 21). The people who rip you off today will be ripping others off in twenty years' time and have nothing to show for it. Remember, it was your own fault in using or choosing them in the first place. While you, on the other hand, will be extremely wealthy even if you only have a few HMOs.

Rule 8
Give respect

You will find it much easier to deal with tenants and others if you are nice to them – even if they do not deserve it. Remember they are your customers. Do not expect respect in return and you will not be disappointed.

Rule 9
Don't expect fair play

In nearly every other sphere of business, if the rules were so one-sided there would be an enormous outcry against the unfairness of it all. Discrimination against landlords is rife and no one cares a damn. At the time of writing, one of the largest landlord associations even appears to be campaigning for more action against bad landlords – yes, I said *against* landlords.

If a tenant wants to they can cause you serious harm, and there is very little you can do about it. You are expected to, and have to follow the law. If your tenants don't, there is little you can usually do apart from evict them. There is no point in suing a person who has no assets, and the only asset most people have is property. As I said in Rule 6, keep your eye on the rewards in the future.

Rule 10
Be nice to tenants

People are very reluctant to sue those who they like. To understand this concept I suggest you read *Blink* by Malcolm Gladwell. On page forty of his book, Gladwell discusses the research done to identify which American doctors are sued.

Analysis of malpractice lawsuits shows that there are highly skilled, competent doctors who get sued a lot, and doctors who make lots of mistakes and never get sued. Gladwell goes on to ask why this is and speaks to medical malpractice lawyers. They all say the same thing: patients will not sue a doctor they like, however incompetent.

Rule 11
Treat non-payment excuses as lies

Treat all excuses for non-payment as lies. The exception is where a claim for housing benefit is being made, as it can take some time for housing benefit payment to be processed (see Rule 29). With the rest of the excuses, they are usually lies. I can assure you that with over twenty years' experience this is inevitably the case, so avoid the grief of believing tenants and then being upset when you discover you have been tricked. This brings me on to my 12th rule.

Rule 12
Serve eviction notice as soon as tenant fails to pay

Serve a Section 8 Notice to Evict as soon as a tenant fails to pay. Evicting tenants is a long-winded process and takes the same period of time if you start immediately or wait months. Don't believe anything said about late payment of rent, as rarely is it correct. Start the eviction process as soon as a tenant misses a payment. It may sound harsh, but I can assure you from long experience that it is the best approach. I have perfected a system that allows me to get a Possession Order against a tenant within nine weeks of the first missed payment, and I have now done over 300 evictions without failure. See my website www.hmodaddy.com for details on my *DIY Eviction* manual and courses.

It costs nothing to start the eviction process and you can stop the process at any time. You can get a Possession Order and still allow the tenant to stay, especially if they start paying the rent and hopefully the arrears – though it is the exception for a tenant to improve their behaviour and pay off their arrears.

Remember Rule 10, and bear in mind Rule 13, so do it nicely. When I serve an eviction notice I am very careful how I go about it and make it look like I am doing the tenants a favour. I often get thanked when I serve an eviction notice.

Rule 13
Retaliatory complaints

Take great care when serving eviction notices as all the

tenant's promises and excuses to pay the rent (which are rarely true) at this point go out of the window. The tenant will then say the reason they have not paid the rent was because they had an accident due to some defect in the premises, which they have continually complained about but which you have never heard about. Or they will say it's due to faults in the property that you know nothing about, but again they will claim that they have complained to you 'for years'.

To avoid this, or reduce the likelihood of it happening, I use a late payment statement where the tenant signs to say they are in arrears and the reason(s) why – along with an opportunity to identify faults or defects. A copy is available in my forms, agreements and letters pack CD/USB, only available from www.hmodaddy.com.

Rule 14
Keep good records

To have a hope of defending yourself in court against a judiciary that is generally hostile towards landlords, you need to have good record keeping. Firstly, ensure all complaints are logged with time, date and details. Take and keep photographic evidence with a date-stamped camera, preferably with the tenant present where appropriate. Patience, tact and negotiation are the tools you need in this situation. NB. The time is not relevant, but it seems to impress judges.

I use a late payment statement (available in my forms, agreements and letters pack CD/USB, only available from www.hmodaddy.com), which the tenant completes and signs to say why the rent is late and acknowledge they are in arrears, and give the reason(s) why along with the opportunity to identify any faults or defects. Too often when I get to court the story changes. The favourite story is that they did not know they were in arrears or they had paid. If the tenant admits in writing at the time what they owe, this reduces the likelihood of them denying they owe rent and diminishes their credibility should they do so.

Rule 15
Tipping point

Prompt and firm chasing up of rent payments will go a long way to reduce bad debts. I estimate that bad debts could be reduced by 80% by acting firmly and quickly. Once a typical HMO tenant is allowed to get over £500 in debt, this is the tipping point. There is little chance they will pay the arrears and they often just leave when chased for payment.

Rule 16
Believe in yourself

You will need self-belief in enormous scoops. Most people have difficulty in believing in themselves – so if you are like the rest of us, you just need to work on excelling in this area. If you do not believe me regarding how insecure we all are, I suggest you attend a personal enlightenment course. Choose someone who you think looks like a confident person and sit next to them. Don't be surprised if before day three you will be holding them while they sob their eyes out telling you how inadequate they are.

My point is: do not rely on anyone. Do not seek the approval of others, and make your own decisions. If property was such an easy idea, everyone would be doing it. So expect more than a fair share of negativity. Your family, friends and colleagues may be your life, but they are very unlikely to support or approve of you being a landlord unless they are landlords themselves – and maybe not even then. Be careful of professionals and be under no illusion that councils are there to support or help you. From long experience I can assure you, you are well and truly on your own in this business. Don't look for understanding from anyone, apart from your dog or cat.

Rule 17
Do research carefully

If you talk to other landlords, assess very carefully what they say. They are unlikely to say, "Go for it!" There are a number of reasons for this, including:

- Most are selfish and do not want to give anything away.
- They are fearful of competition.
- They have had what they feel is a bad time.
- They rarely have much of a clue of what they are doing.

The questions amongst others to ask them are:

- How long have you been operating HMOs?
- What did you buy the property for, and what would it be worth today?
- What proportion of tenants: don't pay; cause problems; go to councils; etc. But don't expect them to be able to work this out, as they are probably innumerate.

A typical conversation I have with an HMO landlord goes a bit like this:

Question: Do you have any HMOs?

Answer: I used to have an HMO, but I got rid of it because I got fed up with tenants not paying, damaging the property, and complaining, etc.

You therefore need to go on and ask more questions such as:

Question: What did you buy the property for?

Answer: It was in the nineties and I inherited it. Then, after a couple of years I sold it.

Question: What would it be worth now?

Answer: I hate to think – at least four times more than what I sold it for.

Question: What would be the rental income?

Answer: I could retire on the income if I had kept it.

The point I am making is that without intelligent questions you would probably have come away with the impression that having an HMO creates a load of problems without understanding any of the benefits.

Rule 18
Never delay dealing with repairs, abandonment or late payment

Do not delay with dealing with repairs, tenants abandonment and late payment. A landlord is in a service industry; you need to look after your tenants. Try to avoid comparing yourself with the social sector – they protect their own and look down on the private rented sector. Look at the social sector service targets for doing repairs online – it takes them months to do things. Do what you can as quickly as you can, otherwise delay will become a habit. Some tenants will appreciate your prompt service while others won't. You can never please everyone. Some will use any excuse to refuse to pay rent, so try to avoid this by acting promptly with repairs.

The same goes with late payment. Unless you show concern about payment, a significant number of your tenants will not. Remember Rule 14 and keep good records of your actions.

Rule 19
"I'll have to ask the boss!"

Use this excuse to consult with your partner, husband or wife. It will give you a barrier to allow yourself time to think, especially when letting. This is an intuitive business. At the upper end of the market you can rely on references, guarantors, etc – but you also need have to rely on intuition, which is often disregarded in this educated, rational world. You need to get your intuition up and working again. Our ancestors very quickly had to assess friend or foe, yet we debunk this skill. Sometimes it takes a bit of time to assess a person or situation, so do not rush it. Give yourself the luxury of time to think and talk it over. You will often be surprised when you think over what would initially seemed to be a reliable prospective tenant, and find that things do not add up.

Rule 20
The rule of 20

After twenty years the original purchase price of the property, which is then converted into an HMO, will be equal or thereabouts to the initial gross rent. For example, a house purchased in 1994 for £30K and turned into an HMO will produce a rent of about £30K per annum today as an HMO. It is rental growth like this that makes this business so good but emphasises that it's a long-term business and not a get rich quick scheme.

Rule 21
Rule of 40/10

After forty years, a house purchased and turned into an HMO will be generating gross rent per annum at about ten times the original purchase price. For example, a house purchased in 1974 for £4,000 and turned into an HMO, will produce a rent today of about £40,000 per annum

I often get asked by people when I explain this rule, "But what if I don't live for another forty years?" My answer is that you don't have to worry. But if you do live to see it, you will be very grateful you invested in HMOs as you will enjoy the phenomenal income. Remember the HMO will need to be refurbished every seven to ten years to keep it up to standard and for ease of letting.

Rule 22
If you want affection get a dog or cat

Do not expect any appreciation, respect or recognition for providing good, low cost, flexible housing, then you will not be disappointed. I spend tens of thousands providing additional facilities for tenants. Then I used to feel surprised and upset when all I got was complaints or abuse that I was a greedy landlord, that I gave nothing, it broke down or they didn't like it. Tenants are loath to give any appreciation to their landlord, as if it's against the rules.

Rule 23
Tenants aren't friends

Don't become friends with tenants, but be friendly. It is a delicate balance. Having a good relationship helps the process, but if some tenants become over familiar they will often take advantage.

Rule 24
Don't employ tenants

Be wary of employing tenants – some of my worst problems have come from doing this. This is probably a lot more to do with me not managing my staff well enough, and taking decisive action when things go wrong. If they are also tenants, it is harder to take action against them.

Superficially, it appears to be a good idea to appoint someone in the HMO to look after it and give them a rent deduction, etc, but in my experience it usually proves to be unsuccessful. The tenant house minder has exploited and/or abused the situation to bully the other tenants or steal rent, etc. If you do use a tenant house minder regularly, check they have done what they say they have, and keep them in line.

Rule 25
Tenants lie about other tenants

Tenants don't always tell the truth about other tenants, so be careful about a tenant who complains about another. Often they are not the victim but the perpetrator. They might say, "So and so hit me" or "they stole from me", etc, when it turns out they were the ones who hit the other tenant or had been stealing. Numerous times a tenant has complained their room has been broken into, only for me to discover that they were the ones who did the breaking in.

Rule 26
Tenants don't complain enough

Tenants, as a rule, rarely report other tenants. Instead, they just leave. Few tenants want to be a grass. Too often I have had a calm and stable house wrecked by one bad tenant, but because I did not realise the problem soon enough or get rid of the bad tenant, I have ended up losing most of the tenants in the house.

Rule 27
Professionals usually have a hidden agenda

Don't expect professionals to act in your interest – professionals so often look upon you as an income stream and may not give the right advice, which is usually not to use them and resolve matters without them. Some will constantly look to cover their liability, so will say you need this investigation or report. This will incur you an unnecessary expense or insurance premiums to cover a potential liability. For example, a valuer refused to accept that an extension obviously built over twenty years ago was immune from planning enforcement, and I was required to take out insurance to cover any possible action by the council. You only need to think of the enormous amount of extra surgical procedures carried out in the USA, where doctors are paid by the operation, compared to the UK where they are not, to realise what has gone wrong.

Unless the government puts strict controls on 'no win no fee' solicitors, we will see an enormous explosion in litigation. The reduction in legal aid will be replaced by legal insurers.

Rule 28
Everything is your responsibility

Accept that everything is the landlord's responsibility – the tenants have responsibility for nothing. I have lost count of the number of tenants who have blamed me for their filthy rooms, even if the rooms were immaculate when they moved in. It is apparently not the tenant's fault that they have not cleaned their room or put out the rubbish. If you want an example of this, see the clip about one of my tenants in the BBC programme *Meet the Landlords* – you can view this on youtube.com.

This attitude will help keep your stress levels down. It does not mean you are liable for everything, it is just that most people seem to think you are to blame for all of society's ills. I have had owner occupiers expecting me to pay for their wind-damaged fences because my adjoining property does not have fence panels to stop the wind blowing their fences down.

Legislators have continually tried to make landlords responsible for their tenants' anti-social behaviour. It is horrendous because landlords do not have any power or resources to do that job.

Rule 29
Housing benefit is difficult

Housing benefit is difficult to deal with – housing benefit is a complex area and it can take months for claims to be processed. If you are going to handle housing benefit tenants, then you need to be aware of what you are letting yourself in for and learn the process of how housing benefit works. Also, be prepared to devote an enormous amount of time to help tenants to make a claim, then chasing up the claim and monitoring the claim. I estimate each housing benefit claim takes an extra eight hours over the life of the claim compared to handling a non-benefit claimant. *Operating Standards* – a manual that gives the procedures for how I operate all aspects of my business – is only available from www.hmodaddy.com. This also gives detailed instructions on how to handle housing benefit claims successfully.

Rule 30
Experts aren't always right

Experts are not always right, so make your own decisions. This is going to be one of the hardest lessons to learn as we are brought up to believe in the so-called experts. Yet they consistently get it wrong. You need to probe why such a decision is made and then evaluate for yourself. Be deeply sceptical if the experts' advice makes money for them or keeps them in a job – good advice and profit are not safe bedfellows.

Rule 31
Avoid litigation

There is so much a tenant can accuse you of and at no cost, trouble or comeback on them. They can bring a frivolous complaint aided by 'no win no fee' solicitors, Citizens' Advice Bureau and other legal bodies. You, on the other hand, have to pay, and pay handsomely, to defend yourself. It is therefore better to avoid such litigation in the first place. If you want some examples of what this can mean for landlords, see my book *HMOs and Compensation for Unlawful Eviction* available from www.hmodaddy.com.

Rule 32
Expect to be scared

The human mind is not very good at assessing risk or reward. Look at how many people play the lottery or smoke. When we are doing something new or unusual, we tend to be very fearful of the unknown and constantly want reassurance. If you ask experts, they will be concerned about their liability – so they paint a cautionary picture, so that you do not come back and sue them. The result is that you spend a lot of money on obtaining expert advice and end up not doing anything. Learn to face your fear and still take action.

Rule 33
Get it in writing

Get everything in writing. Council and other officials have been known to lie or misrepresent what they have said. If the advice they give is to your advantage, get them to put it in writing or *you* confirm what was said in writing, and have proof of sending. Email and faxes are good for this, though emails are far better. Most of the time you can rely on what is said, but if the officials have not put it in writing then it is easy to dispute what was said.

Often officials make it up as they go and will not commit themselves to writing, which means you may choose to take no notice. Don't push this rule too far – certain officials want an easy life. If they feel they can have a little chat with you and the issues are sorted out, then that may be best for all parties. If it is in writing it is official, and if you do not respond or comply, you are leaving yourself wide open.

Rule 34
Treat officials with respect

Know the rules, but play dumb. I have said for a long time, "What is the use of housing standard officials?" but I am not going to change the world.* They have enormous power and can destroy your business at a whim. Don't get them focusing on you, which they can if you upset them. The fighting back approach may work, if you make the official's life hell by complaining, appealing, etc, they may become very reluctant to engage with you again.

What officials focus on rarely makes sense, improves safety or is wanted by the tenants. Placate them and they will often ignore 90% of the issues they could have also picked on. Even if you have had a brand-new property, you will understand that they have their problems as well. It is almost impossible not to find faults with a building. Send two officials to a property and they will often find two sets of faults and give contradictory advice. Sometimes it is better to do what they want if it doesn't cost much. It is all a game.

*For more information, read my book *HMO Daddy Reveals All*, available from www.hmodaddy.com.

Rule 35
Hone your intuition

Use and hone your intuition – being a landlord is a people business. You have to deal with one of the most difficult, complex and contradictory things there are: people. Letting agents have produced very refined ways of assessing tenants, but unfortunately these almost fail-safe processes (i.e. job references, bank statements, credit score, guarantees, etc) only apply to less than 50% of the rental market. For example, less than 10% of DSS tenants have bank accounts or can provide qualified guarantors, so you may need to use other ways to assess your tenants. Once you have done what you can check, ask lots of questions then try to verify the answers and use your intuition.

Intuition has been under-rated in our rational scientific society. We all have it, but often fail to use it. Understand you can improve your intuition if you use it. Some people are more intuitive than others, so whenever you can, get them involved in the selection of tenants. I have stated the ways I check both working and DSS tenants in *Operating Standards* (a manual that states the procedure on how I operate all aspect of my business) available from www.hmodaddy.com.

Rule 36
The truth will out

Though I do not expect much from tenants I am continually surprised at how often tenants will tell me things, stand up for fair play and are generally truthful. If you have an allegation that you suspect is wrong, do not be afraid to listen to your tenants. The truth will always come out.

Rule 37
Energy conservation is a con

Treat all claims of energy efficiency, savings, etc, as a con and you will not go far wrong. The snake oil salesmen have moved into this industry aided by the government. I pay the bills in over a hundred of my HMOs and have not found that any of it works in practice. For more on this read my book *HMO Daddy Reveals All,* available from www.hmodaddy.com.

Rule 38
Manage your HMOs yourself

Novice HMO landlords are often nervous about managing HMOs. But providing you are reasonably close to where you live or operate, you like people, and you believe as a landlord you should provide a service, then you are the best person to manage your HMO. Rarely will anyone else take the care and attention that you will. On top of this, you will make a lot more money as not only will your HMO be more effectively run, but also you save on the cost of employing others. Once an HMO is set up, it takes very little effort or time to run. Minor repairs, which an agent will charge a lot to sort out, can be done by yourself. You will soon learn how to do all kinds of repairs.

Landlords often refer to 'the midnight call' and how to cope. An agent is not going to do anything at that time of night either, so don't worry. Also, remember that, generally, agents will pass problems back to you to solve.

Rule 39
Give bad tenants their money back

A bad tenant only becomes worse. So if you have discovered that you made a bad decision or that the tenant does not fit in, then give the tenant all their money back, providing they leave immediately. It will be far cheaper in the long run – better than losing all the other tenants and ongoing problems. You need to ensure that the tenant leaves and hands back the keys. You don't want any comebacks or allegations of wrongful eviction. To cover myself, I get the tenant to sign to say they have left voluntarily. See my HMO forms, agreements and letters manual + CD/USB only available from www.hmodaddy.com.

Rule 40
If it's free, it is abused

Sadly, there is a significant minority who will take advantage of anything that is free. If you provide unlimited central heating, they will put it on full blast and open the windows. If the electricity is also included, they will use an electric heater at the same time. If the washing machine is provided, they do their washing one item at a time and so on. The answer is not to provide it or to meter it. Fair use policies have little effect on most of these abusers as they do not believe they should have to pay, or they refuse to pay, and it is unfair on the other tenants.

Rule 41
Forget maintenance contracts

Don't waste money on maintenance contracts – maintenance contracts, insurance, breakdown cover, etc, rarely pay for themselves. If it was any good, why would businesses sell it as it would not make them money? Gas boiler cover is the main culprit. You could buy a new boiler every three years for what you pay for the insurance. It may be worth paying extra and buying a boiler with a seven- or ten-year warranty rather than paying for an annual maintenance contract.

Rule 42
Fit a fire door

Fire doors are remarkably cheap (about £25 from Howdens

Joinery, www.howdens.com) and represent good value in that they are far stronger than most ordinary doors and give better sound-proofing. Your local authorities may not insist that you fit fire doors in your HMO, but in case they change their mind, you will already have them fitted.

Rule 43
Extras make no difference

All those extras make no difference. I am sorry to say that I have found no evidence that providing bedding, crockery, co-ordinating colours, central heating, flat screen TV, etc, makes very much difference. I know this makes no sense, logic would say otherwise – and yes, I know most of my readers will vehemently object to this.

I have had this conversation time and time again and have had usually, middle-class HMO landladies screaming at me that I talk nonsense. What they are really saying is that their pride won't allow them to provide anything less than what they would want to live in themselves, and let's accept it as that. I estimate that billions are wasted by such landlords on nothing more than vanity and fear they will not be able to let their property if they drop their standards. Yes, the tenants will take the extras and say they like it. But it is not something they are prepared to pay for, and as a business this is what matters. In other words, all these extras make no difference as to whether they take the property. The only exception may be broadband, where I believe but have no evidence (in fact, the contrary) that it makes a difference. Prospective tenants will ask if we have broadband, and when we say the property does not have it, they sigh but still take the room.

Rule 44
Finding tenants

The key to getting tenants is to, wherever possible, respond to enquiries immediately. Be welcoming, enthusiastic, flexible and have clean, fresh, nice-smelling, warm and newly decorated rooms. Prospective tenants will often call though a list of properties that are listed as available and take the property of the first landlord to answer providing it is acceptable.

With all tenants be careful and ask questions. Check where you can and use your intuition. Avoid, if in doubt.

Rule 45
Do not show more than two rooms or properties

It sounds counter-intuitive, but in my experience almost

everyone who sees more than two rooms never takes anything. But worse, it wastes an enormous amount of your time. Typically when I let a room, the prospective tenant walks in, has a quick look around, may ask a few questions, and say, "Yep, this will do – how do I pay?"

Rule 46
The longer a tenant stays, the longer they will stay

I find there is a lot of turnover in the first few months of the average tenant's stay, and turnover slows down after six months. I guestimate over 60% of my tenants will leave in the first month or two. If a tenant stays three months, there is a better than fifty-fifty chance they will stay for six months. If they stay for six months, they are likely to stay for another twelve months. If they stay for twelve months they will stay for years.

Rule 47
Charge an administration fee

Most letting agents charge an administration fee, yet very few landlords do. Before the Tenancy Deposit Scheme came in, I had reviewed the scheme and rejected taking deposits as being a potential liability. Sadly, events have proved me right. Luckily, few tenants have taken the opportunity to sue their landlords for the deposit, plus three times the original deposit, which many could if they only realised the opportunity. Also see my article 'How to Avoid the Tenancy Deposit Scheme and Turn it into a Marketing and Financial Advantage' now re-published in my new book *HMO Daddy Reveals All*, available from www.hmodaddy.com. So instead of bothering with a deposit, charge an administration fee that you can keep. Make sure you clearly state it is an administration fee and it is not refundable. I charge £175 administration fee for a studio, and I know of those who charge far more.

Rule 48
Do not increase rents for good tenants

Generally speaking, keep the tenants you have as the longer they stay, the longer they will stay (see Rule 46). A rent increase will encourage them to review whether they wish to continue as your tenant. If a tenant leaves this will result in you having a void, cost in time and expense in finding a new tenant, cleaning and possible redecorating costs.

Rule 49
Increase rent for problem tenants

If you have a problem tenant, you can bring home to them their inconvenience by substantially increasing their rent. This may go towards compensating you for the extra work such tenants cause you and send a warning to other tenants. You will probably find that the other tenants may appreciate you doing this as if a tenant is a problem to you then they will be a problem for others as well.

Increased rent has to be done properly, otherwise they can be successfully challenged. I deal with how to increase rents in my manual *DIY Eviction*, available from www.hmodaddy.com.

Rule 50
Do not charge a deposit

I don't charge a deposit. I stopped doing so months before the Tenancy Deposit Scheme (TDS) started. I looked at the TDS and it made me review why I took deposits. See '12 Ways to Avoid the Tenant Deposit Scheme and Turn It into a Marketing Advantage' in my book *HMO Daddy Reveals All*, available from www.hmodaddy.com. Instead, I charge an administration fee (see Rule 47). Deposits require enormous administration, have draconian penalties if you slip up, and make enormous profits for those who operate the scheme. It is not a problem to make a profit, but see Rule 27. Would the organisations that make so much money out of the scheme be so supportive of it if they made nothing?

Charging deposits is worse than useless at the bottom end of the market. The tenant simply does not pay the last month's rent and it is a barrier to letting. I have grave doubts as to the efficacy of deposits in the professional market, where tenants want the ability to get a reference so would take care regardless of any deposit. You can charge your tenants for damage caused, especially if it is in the terms of your agreement. I put such terms in my agreements – see my forms, agreements and letters manual + CD/USB only available from www.hmodaddy.com.

The Author

HMO Daddy, Jim Haliburton, is a star of the BBC show *Meet the Landlords*, author of over ten books and manuals, including *How to Become a Multi-Millionaire HMO Landlord*, and regularly writes articles for property magazines.

He began investing in property in 1991, letting rooms to students, while he was a college law lecturer.

In 2004 he decided to leave his job and buy investment properties full-time. He now owns a letting office as well as over 100 HMOs, thirty single-lets and twenty-four Rent-to-Rents.

He is also in regular demand as a speaker at property meetings around the UK and runs courses and mentorships on the business of being an HMO landlord. He is unique in the business in that he lets people work in his property business to learn the skills of being an HMO landlord and gives tours of his properties.

I want to hear from you

As a reader of my guide you are the most important critic and commentator. I value your opinion and comments, and want to know what else you would like me to include in the guide. Please let me know if you disagree with any of my advice, and offer any other words of wisdom you wish to make.

I welcome your comments. You can email, call or write to me to let me know what you did or did not like about my guide as well as what I can do to make it better or what other information or service I could provide. Please note that I am often difficult to contact by phone because, as you can appreciate, I am very busy. When I get a few spare minutes I love to talk about the business, so please do not be offended if I say, "Call back or leave a message."

I also provide training courses on such things as evictions as well as how to acquire, get finance, convert and run HMOs, which you can find out about on my website www.hmodaddy.com.

When you write to me, please include your name, email address, home address and phone number. I assure you, I will value and review your comments.

Email: jim@hmodaddy.com

Website: www.hmodaddy.com

Mail: Jim Haliburton
            14 Walsall Road
            Wednesbury
            WS10 9JL

Phone: 09131-300054
            Calls cost £1.50 per minute